Zak is Off!

by Abbie Rushton
Illustrated by Erin Taylor

OXFORD
UNIVERSITY PRESS

Zak

Zak in his kit.

Zak has to go!

Zak runs. He is fit.

jacket

hat

Zak gets his kit on.

Zak is off.

Quick, Zak!

It is wet.

I hit the rocks!

Zak can not get to the rocks.

Zak will not quit.

bag

"Get it!" yells Zak.

Yes! She gets the bag.

Zak tugs the bag in.

Zak gets a pat on the back.

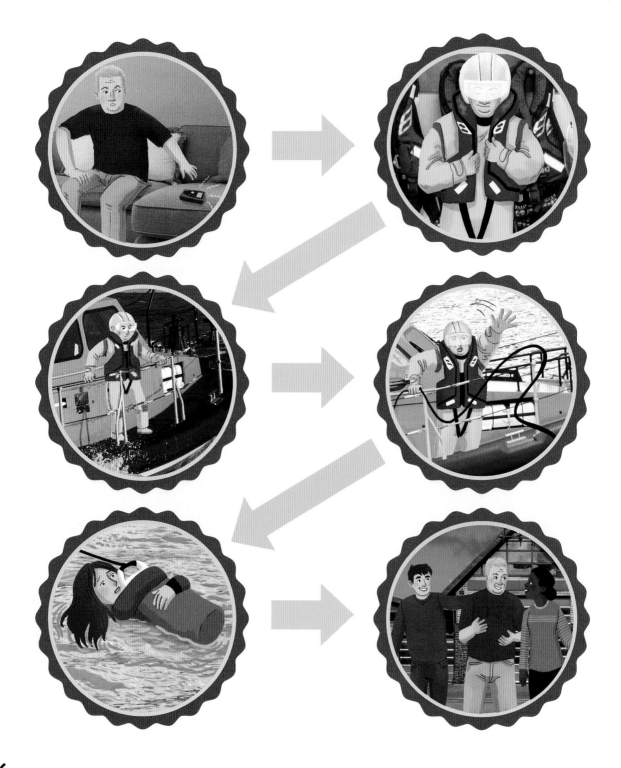